Fantasy & Nature Coloring Book

By Erin Ewer

THIS BOOK INCLUDES 26 SINGLE SIDED COLORING PAGES BY FANTASY ARTIST ERIN EWER.

As an artist, one of my creative goals has always been to use my artwork as a way to share, communicate, and identify with others. I create with the hope that the magic I feel while doing so can also be felt by those who appreciate my work.

With my coloring books I aspire to take that shared experience one step further by blending the boundaries between artist and viewer, and sharing in the creative process. Color brings life to everything it touches; it can be used as a form of expression, as well as a tool for relaxation. Color can excite, frighten, motivate, and thrill.

This book is an invitation for you to create an expression, however you desire to do so. I believe that true magic isn't something you can find deep in an old forest or tucked inside a fairy circle, but something you find within yourself. Open your heart to find your inspiration and let it flow onto the pages, creating a beautiful and magical expression that only you can help breathe life into. ~*Erin*

SEE THE COLORS THE ARTIST CHOSE TO USE
WWW.LIQUIDFAE.COM

Liquid Fae Studios

If markers are used in this coloring book, be sure to insert a blank piece of paper behind the coloring page in order to avoid bleed-through.

Fantasy and Nature Coloring Book
by Erin Ewer
Published by Liquid Fae Studios 2017
ISBN: 978-1-387-48456-0

All images depicted in the book are ©Erin Ewer 2000 - 2017 reproduction in part or in whole is prohibited.

Made in the USA
Monee, IL
04 February 2022